Blessed *are those who* Mourn

Blessed are those who Mourn

*Personalized Prayers
of the Faithful
for the Funeral Rite*

George C. Michalek
and Barbara M. Fader

AVE MARIA PRESS   Notre Dame, Indiana 46556

© 1998 by George C. Michalek and Barbara M. Fader

All rights reserved. No part of this book may be used or reproduced in any manner whatsoever except in the case of reprints in the context of reviews, without written permission from Ave Maria Press, Inc., Notre Dame, IN 46556.

International Standard Book Number: 0-87793-654-4

Cover and text design by Brian Conley

Printed and bound in the United States of America.

Library of Congress Cataloging-in-Publication Data

Michalek, George C.

    Blessed are those who mourn : personalized prayers of the faithful for the funeral rite / George C. Michalek, Barbara M. Fader.

       p.   cm.

    Includes indexes.

    ISBN 0-87793-654-4

    1. Catholic Church. Order of Christian funerals. 2. Funeral service—Catholic Church—Liturgy—Texts. 3. Pastoral prayers. I. Fader, Barbara M.   II. Title.

    BX2035.6.F853M53   1998

    264′.025—dc21

                                   98-4034

                                      CIP

Dedicated to

the ones who comfort those who mourn,
in memory of

Charles and Olga Sayles

and

Ralph, Elinor, and Mark DeGrand.

Contents

Introduction

When we deal with our human mortality, we face what applies not only to all of us, but to each of us. Death is not only universal, it is also most personal. In our mortality we share a common bond with all who have gone before us and will come after us. But much more than a common bond for all humanity, death is a deeply personal separation from those we hold most dear. Death is not only a condition with us from time immemorial, it is also an event very specifically here and now.

Times of loss and grief may cause those who mourn to be particularly sensitive and vulnerable to various expressions of word and action, even though at the same time they may seem to be numb and oblivious to what is happening around them. Ironically, those who minister to the bereaved often discover that they have less opportunity than they would like to prepare sensitive and meaningful funeral liturgies.

The revised *Order of Christian Funerals,* which was approved for use in the United States in 1987, has been of great assistance to priests, deacons, and lay ministers who offer the church's care for those in mourning. Not only does it provide a complete order of prayer for the wake, the funeral Mass, and the committal, it offers texts specially suited to the age and state in life of the deceased.

It is in that spirit of personal, pastoral care that we offer *Blessed Are Those Who Mourn.* The prayers provided here are designed to supplement the nine sets of general intercessions offered in the *Order of Christian Funerals* and to further personalize the wake, funeral, or committal service. They are offered to help those who prepare funeral liturgies and enhance the experience of the bereaved by:

- preserving the sense of uniqueness of the individual and his or her eternal relationship with God by touching upon some specific characteristics of the deceased;
- suggesting the continuity between temporal and eternal life by connecting qualities of the deceased individual's earthly life with some traditional Christian images of eternal life;
- enabling the prayers of the faithful to be more readily integrated with reflections on the deceased and his or her gifts of self to friends, family, and the broader community, which may have been offered in the homily;
- in some instances, referring to verses of scripture which may add depth and meaning;
- giving additional variety to the repertory of intercessory prayers, especially for the sake of those who frequently attend, preside, or serve at funeral liturgies;
- providing models for composing other funeral liturgy intercessions.

How to Use This Book

Blessed Are Those Who Mourn is organized in this way: Part One provides prayers relating to the characteristics of the deceased, and Part Two offers prayers based on the readings from the lectionary for funerals. Each part has subsections that gather prayers which relate, for example, to the key relationships in the life of the deceased or to the gospel readings in the lectionary. The prayers are numbered consecutively and indexed by those numbers so that they may be easily located.

We suggest that you use the intercessions in this book in concert with those provided in the *Order of Christian Funerals*. Appendix A provides a form which enables you to gather together the prayers you select so that the minister may easily read from one sheet rather than having to move about in the two books to find the appropriate prayers.

We have also provided a computer disk which contains all the intercessions. We recommend that you transcribe the intercessions from the *Order of Christian Funerals* onto this disk so that you have all the possible selections in one place. This will enable you to easily gather the selected prayers into one document that can be printed in a highly readable format.

The files on this disk are saved in Rich Text File (RTF) format, a sort of "generic" format. In order to use this disk, you must have a computer and word processing software which allow you to access it. Either a Macintosh or Macintosh-compatible computer, or an IBM or IBM-compatible computer will be able to open the files. (If you have a Macintosh computer which is several years old, it may *not* be able to open the disk.) Most word processing programs will then be able to access the information.

If you are already using *Through Death to Life* by Fr. Joseph M. Champlin (also published by Ave Maria Press) to involve the family in planning the liturgy, *Blessed Are Those Who Mourn* can be used easily alongside it. Simply provide the family with a copy of this book and instruct them to write the numbers of the intercessions they wish to use on the selection form in *Through Death to Life*. Part II of the form provides a space to note which set of general intercessions the family has chosen. Instruct them to write the numbers of these prayers in the space alongside of this. You will then have to integrate these prayers with those selected from *Through Death to Life*.

We have discovered that the use of such supplementary intercessions during the prayers of the faithful touches the need of those who mourn to grieve their loved ones in a very personal way and speaks to the desire of those who prepare the liturgy to do so in a very caring way. We hope that they will be helpful to you.

Fr. George C. Michalek
Barbara M. Fader

Part One

Prayers Relating to Characteristics of the Deceased Person

Relationship to Family and Friends

1

Little Child

1. During his/her life, *name* showed us the childlike qualities of trust and love. May he/she now be held in the loving arms of God, our Father.

      We pray to the Lord . . . Lord, hear our prayer.

or   Lord, in your mercy . . . Hear our prayer.

2. *Name's* family cherished him/her as being blameless and full of love. May we mirror these qualities in our own lives as children of God.

      We pray to the Lord . . . Lord, hear our prayer.

or   Lord, in your mercy . . . Hear our prayer.

3. You have allowed us to hold *name* for a little while. Help us now to entrust him/her to you, knowing that there is no more tender love than that which is found in your arms.

      We pray to the Lord . . . Lord, hear our prayer.

or   Lord, in your mercy . . . Hear our prayer.

      (based on Mk 10:13-16)

4. *Parent's name* and *parent's name* called *child's name* THEIR child during his/her short time with us. May they be consoled in knowing that he/she is also one of God's beloved children.

      We pray to the Lord . . . Lord, hear our prayer.

or   Lord, in your mercy . . . Hear our prayer.

      (based on 1 Jn 3:1-2)

See also prayers 241-243; if the child was non-baptized, see prayers 244-246.

Older Child/Adolescent

5. *Name* could look forward to a life filled with much promise. May he/she now know the fulfillment of the promise of eternal life.

      We pray to the Lord . . . Lord, hear our prayer.

or   Lord, in your mercy . . . Hear our prayer.

6. *Name* has been raised to eternal life; may we be strengthened in our faith and look forward to being reunited with him/her in our eternal home.

>We pray to the Lord . . . Lord, hear our prayer.
>
>*or*   Lord, in your mercy . . . Hear our prayer.

7. We saw *name*, like the young Jesus of Nazareth, grow in wisdom and grace. May we look forward to our reunion with him/her before God's throne.

>We pray to the Lord . . . Lord, hear our prayer.
>
>*or*   Lord, in your mercy . . . Hear our prayer.
>
>(based on Lk 2:52)

Spouse

8. May God grant *deceased spouse's name* the prize of heaven for his/her faithful love of his wife/her husband, *surviving spouse's name*.

>We pray to the Lord . . . Lord, hear our prayer.
>
>*or*   Lord, in your mercy . . . Hear our prayer.

9. During their long marriage, *name* and *name* entrusted their hearts to one another. May we join *surviving spouse's name* in now entrusting his/her life partner to the Lord.

>We pray to the Lord . . . Lord, hear our prayer.
>
>*or*   Lord, in your mercy . . . Hear our prayer.
>
>(based on Prv 31:1)

10. *Surviving spouse's name* looked to *deceased spouse's name* for strength and support. May *surviving spouse's name* receive the strength and support he/she now needs from God and this community of faith.

>We pray to the Lord . . . Lord, hear our prayer.
>
>*or*   Lord, in your mercy . . . Hear our prayer.

11. In their marriage, *deceased spouse's name* mirrored God's faithful love for *surviving spouse's name*. May he/she *[deceased spouse]* now experience the fullness of that faithful love in heaven.

We pray to the Lord . . . Lord, hear our prayer.
or   Lord, in your mercy . . . Hear our prayer.

Parent or Grandparent

12. As a parent, *name* taught his/her children to pray. May the prayers of his/her children bring him/her to the throne of God.

We pray to the Lord . . . Lord, hear our prayer.
or   Lord, in your mercy . . . Hear our prayer.

13. As *name* shared his/her faith with his/her children [and grand-children] by word and deed, may he/she now experience the fulfillment of that faith in union with you forever.

We pray to the Lord . . . Lord, hear our prayer.
or   Lord, in your mercy . . . Hear our prayer.
        (based on 2 Tm 1:3-5)

14. With his/her family, *name* put others first. May this sacrificial love now be rewarded by Christ, who gave himself up for us.

We pray to the Lord . . . Lord, hear our prayer.
or   Lord, in your mercy . . . Hear our prayer.

15. *Name* gave the gift of love to his/her family. May he/she now receive the eternal gift of God's love.

We pray to the Lord . . . Lord, hear our prayer.
or   Lord, in your mercy . . . Hear our prayer.

16. During his/her life, *name* provided for his/her family; may he/she now enjoy the eternal reward provided for him/her by God.

We pray to the Lord . . . Lord, hear our prayer.
or   Lord, in your mercy . . . Hear our prayer.

Foster Parent

17. *Name* shared his/her home and love with those who were taken from their homes of origin. May he/she now be welcomed with love into his/her eternal home.

     We pray to the Lord . . . Lord, hear our prayer.
or   Lord, in your mercy . . . Hear our prayer

Adult Family Member

18. In this life, *name* was a "Martha" for the Lord, serving the practical needs of others. May he/she now also be blessed with the portion given to Mary.

     We pray to the Lord . . . Lord, hear our prayer.
or   Lord, in your mercy . . . Hear our prayer.
     (based on Lk 10:38-42)

19. As *name* gave so much of himself/herself to those he/she loved, may he/she now receive the bounty of eternal joy from the hands of Christ.

     We pray to the Lord . . . Lord, hear our prayer.
or   Lord, in your mercy . . . Hear our prayer.

Senior Citizen

20. *Name* devoted much of his/her retirement to his/her relationship with God. May he/she now be blessed with the fruition of that friendship.

     We pray to the Lord . . . Lord, hear our prayer.
or   Lord, in your mercy . . . Hear our prayer.

21. Change was a constant companion in *name's* long journey. May we now accept his/her last change, from mortality to immortality.

     We pray to the Lord . . . Lord, hear our prayer.
or   Lord, in your mercy . . . Hear our prayer.
     (based on 1 Cor 15:51-54)

22. *Name* dedicated much of his/her latter years to building up the *[specify, if desired]* Christian community. May he/she now enjoy the companionship of the saints in heaven.

   We pray to the Lord . . . Lord, hear our prayer.
or Lord, in your mercy . . . Hear our prayer.
   See also prayer 139.

Caregiver

For a Caregiver Who Has Died

23. During his/her life, *name* lovingly and faithfully cared for others *[or specify a person]* ; now may he/she know the wonderful bounty of God's loving care for him/her.

   We pray to the Lord . . . Lord, hear our prayer.
or Lord, in your mercy . . . Hear our prayer.

For a Caregiver Who Survives the Deceased

24. Caring for *deceased's name* was a large part of *caregiver's name's* life; we pray for *caregiver's name* that he/she may now release *deceased's name* into God's tender care.

   We pray to the Lord . . . Lord, hear our prayer.
or Lord, in your mercy . . . Hear our prayer.

Friend Born in a Foreign Land

25. *Name* trusted much in God's care when he/she came from *[specify place]* _____ to live among us. May we now entrust our friend into his/her new homeland in heaven.

   We pray to the Lord . . . Lord, hear our prayer.
or Lord, in your mercy . . . Hear our prayer.
   (based on Is 41:9-10)

Special Friend

26. Sirach describes a faithful friend as a sturdy shelter. We pray for *name's* special friends, who found him/her to be a sturdy shelter, that they may take comfort in God who shelters us all.

     We pray to the Lord . . . Lord, hear our prayer.

or   Lord, in your mercy . . . Hear our prayer.

     (based on Sir 6:14-17)

     See also prayers 192-193.

Vocation or Avocation

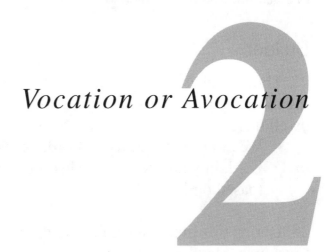

Builder

Business Owner

Clerical or Support Staff

Doctor

Farmer

Fine or Applied Artist

Health or Mental Health Services Provider

Homemaker

Judge

Laborer/One Who Performed Strenuous Work

Lawyer

Police, Fire, or Emergency Worker

Public Servant or Government Employee

Salesperson

Scholar or Scientist

Teacher or Professor

Traveler/One Whose Work Involved Frequent Travel

Veteran

Writer

Builder

27. Through his/her profession as a builder, *name* provided housing for many people. Now may he/she come into God's house and dwell there forever.
> We pray to the Lord . . . Lord, hear our prayer.

or　Lord, in your mercy . . . Hear our prayer.
> (based on Ps 23:6)

28. During this life, *name* built many structures on sturdy foundations; now may he/she receive the reward of a life built on Jesus, the Rock of faith.
> We pray to the Lord . . . Lord, hear our prayer.

or　Lord, in your mercy . . . Hear our prayer.
> (based on Mt 7:24-25)

Business Owner

29. As *name* served the community in the *[specify]* _____ business, may his/her service now be honored in the community of the saints.
> We pray to the Lord . . . Lord, hear our prayer.

or　Lord, in your mercy . . . Hear our prayer.

Clerical or Support Staff

30. *Name* worked as a/n *[specify occupation]* _____, contributing his/her talents to serve and support others. May he/she now enter into the joy of his/her Master.
> We pray to the Lord . . . Lord, hear our prayer.

or　Lord, in your mercy . . . Hear our prayer.
> (based on Mt 25:14-15, 19-21)

Doctor

31. In life, people came to *name* seeking healing; now as he/she comes into the presence of God, may he/she experience the love from which all healing comes.
> We pray to the Lord . . . Lord, hear our prayer.

or   Lord, in your mercy . . . Hear our prayer.

32. *Name* extended help and comfort to those suffering from illness; may he/she now know the powerful compassion of the Divine Physician.
> We pray to the Lord . . . Lord, hear our prayer.

or   Lord, in your mercy . . . Hear our prayer.

Farmer

33. *Name* lived close to the earth. He/she watched the coming of the seasons and the passing of the years with their sowing and sprouting, ripening and harvesting. May he/she now present to God the good harvest of his/her life.
> We pray to the Lord . . . Lord, hear our prayer.

or   Lord, in your mercy . . . Hear our prayer.
> (based on Mk 4:26-29)

34. *Name* lived with faith in the mystery of growth and trust in the renewal of the seasons. Grant that we may live with faith in life beyond death and trust in the eternal renewal of your love.
> We pray to the Lord . . . Lord, hear our prayer.

or   Lord, in your mercy . . . Hear our prayer.
> *See also prayer 231.*

Fine or Applied Artist

35. *Name's [specify art form]* _____ illustrated for us the beauty of God's creation; may he/she now exult in the unfading splendor of eternal glory.
> We pray to the Lord . . . Lord, hear our prayer.

or   Lord, in your mercy . . . Hear our prayer.

36. Through *name's* art, we saw the creative spark come alive; may he/she now rejoice in being near to God, the Source of the creative fire.

>We pray to the Lord . . . Lord, hear our prayer.
>
>*or*   Lord, in your mercy . . . Hear our prayer.

Health or Mental Health Services Provider

37. On earth, in his/her service as a/n *[specify occupation]* _____, *name* saw you and loved you in the faces of the troubled, sick, and grieving. Now may he/she have the joy of seeing you and loving you face to face in heaven.

>We pray to the Lord . . . Lord, hear our prayer.
>
>*or*   Lord, in your mercy . . . Hear our prayer.
>
>(based on 1 Cor 13:12)

Homemaker

38. *Name* devoted himself/herself to making a home for those he/she loved. Grant him/her now a place of honor in your heavenly dwelling.

>We pray to the Lord . . . Lord, hear our prayer.
>
>*or*   Lord, in your mercy . . . Hear our prayer.

39. *Name's* home was a welcome refuge and haven for friends and family. Now, as he/she comes home to you, enfold him/her in your loving embrace.

>We pray to the Lord . . . Lord, hear our prayer.
>
>*or*   Lord, in your mercy . . . Hear our prayer.

Judge

40. In this life, *name* sat in judgment receiving the testimony of those who came as witnesses before him/her. May he/she now stand honorably before God, the Judge of the living and the dead, as witness to his/her own life in Christ.

We pray to the Lord . . . Lord, hear our prayer.

or   Lord, in your mercy . . . Hear our prayer.

(based on Acts 10:42-43)

Laborer/One Who Performed Strenuous Work

See prayers 179-180.

Lawyer

41. As *name* brought cases before earthly judges, may he/she now bring evidence before the Divine Judge that during life he/she acted justly, loved tenderly, and walked humbly with our God.

We pray to the Lord . . . Lord, hear our prayer.

or   Lord, in your mercy . . . Hear our prayer.

(based on Mi 6:8, JB)

Police, Fire, or Emergency Worker

42. As *name* sought to protect others, may he/she now know the protection of God's holy presence.

We pray to the Lord . . . Lord, hear our prayer.

or   Lord, in your mercy . . . Hear our prayer.

43. *Name* was a keeper of the peace; may he/she now experience the peace of eternal bliss.

We pray to the Lord . . . Lord, hear our prayer.

or   Lord, in your mercy . . . Hear our prayer.

44. Daily, *name* risked laying down his/her life for others; grant him/her now the fullness of joy that comes from Christ's laying down his life for us.

We pray to the Lord . . . Lord, hear our prayer.

or   Lord, in your mercy . . . Hear our prayer.

(based on Jn 15:13)

45. As in the story of Daniel's friends in the fiery furnace, *name* was challenged to walk into the heart of the flames and be protected by God. May God's protection surround *name's* family at this time of grief.

> We pray to the Lord . . . Lord, hear our prayer.

or   Lord, in your mercy . . . Hear our prayer.
> (based on Dn 3)
> *See also prayers 128-129.*

Public Servant or Government Employee

46. Jesus said, "Anyone who wants to become great among you must be your servant." *Name* imitated Christ in serving others, through *[specify work or agency]*_____; may he/she now share in the greatness of the Lord in his heavenly kingdom.

> We pray to the Lord . . . Lord, hear our prayer.

or   Lord, in your mercy . . . Hear our prayer.
> (based on Mk 10:42-44, JB)

47. In life, *name* participated in governing and exercising authority in the name of the common good; may he/she now enjoy the greatest good, the kingdom of heaven.

> We pray to the Lord . . . Lord, hear our prayer.

or   Lord, in your mercy . . . Hear our prayer.

Salesperson

48. *Name* found challenge and vitality in his/her work in sales; may he/she now find new delight in God's embrace.

> We pray to the Lord . . . Lord, hear our prayer.

or   Lord, in your mercy . . . Hear our prayer.

Scholar or Scientist

49. In his/her work as a/n *[specify]*_____, *name* grew to know and be in awe of God's universe. May he/she now experience the wonder of knowing the wisdom of God's design.

      We pray to the Lord . . . Lord, hear our prayer.
or   Lord, in your mercy . . . Hear our prayer.
      (based on Wis 7:15-21)

Teacher or Professor

50. May *name*, who devoted his/her life to teaching others, now sit with joy at the feet of Jesus, our Teacher.

      We pray to the Lord . . . Lord, hear our prayer.
or   Lord, in your mercy . . . Hear our prayer.

51. Like Christ, the Great Teacher, *name* taught not only by word but by example; grant that we might honor him/her by emulating his/her example and following him/her into God's holy presence.

      We pray to the Lord . . . Lord, hear our prayer.
or   Lord, in your mercy . . . Hear our prayer.
      (based on 1 Tm 4:12-13, 16)
      See also prayer 93.

Traveler/One Whose Work Involved Frequent Travel

52. *Name* has completed his/her travels and come to the end of his/her earthly pilgrimage. Greet him/her with your joyful love and welcome him/her home to the land of light and peace.

      We pray to the Lord . . . Lord, hear our prayer.
or   Lord, in your mercy . . . Hear our prayer.

Veteran

53. *Name* served his/her country in the armed forces to protect the values of freedom and justice; may he/she now enjoy the eternal freedom won for us by Christ.

> We pray to the Lord . . . Lord, hear our prayer.

or　Lord, in your mercy . . . Hear our prayer.
> (based on Rom 8:18-21)

Writer

54. *Name's* tool was the written word; may he/she now exult with Christ, the Eternal Word spoken by the Father.

> We pray to the Lord . . . Lord, hear our prayer.

or　Lord, in your mercy . . . Hear our prayer.
> (based on Jn 1:14)

55. *Name* sought to express meaning through words; may he/she now enjoy the inexpressible fullness of God's love, the source of all meaning.

> We pray to the Lord . . . Lord, hear our prayer.

or　Lord, in your mercy . . . Hear our prayer.

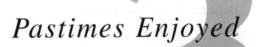

Pastimes Enjoyed

Camping

Collecting

Dancing

Entertaining/Celebrating Special Events

Games, Activities, and Sports

Gardening

Hand Crafts

Reading

Camping

56. *Name* spent many nights on earth in the temporary dwelling of a tent; now may he/she spend eternity in the eternal dwelling of God's heaven.

      We pray to the Lord . . . Lord, hear our prayer.
or   Lord, in your mercy . . . Hear our prayer.
      (based on 2 Cor 5:1-2)

Collecting

57. In collecting *[specify]* _____, *name* found much delight. May he/she now discover the treasure of everlasting joy.

      We pray to the Lord . . . Lord, hear our prayer.
or   Lord, in your mercy . . . Hear our prayer.

Dancing

58. *Name* loved to *[specify]*_____. Now may he/she dance in the embrace of God forever.

      We pray to the Lord . . . Lord, hear our prayer.
or   Lord, in your mercy . . . Hear our prayer.

Entertaining/Celebrating Special Events

59. *Name* loved to *[specify]* _____. May he/she now be caught up in the celebration of celestial joy.

      We pray to the Lord . . . Lord, hear our prayer.
or   Lord, in your mercy . . . Hear our prayer.

Games, Activities, and Sports

Games

60. May the enjoyment that *name* found in playing *[specify game]* _____ be a foreshadowing of his/her happiness in heaven.

      We pray to the Lord . . . Lord, hear our prayer.
or   Lord, in your mercy . . . Hear our prayer.

Activities

61. Jesus said, "I came so that they might have life and have it more abundantly." *Name* found an abundance of life in *[specify activity]*_____. May he/she now exult in the greater abundance of eternal life.

    We pray to the Lord . . . Lord, hear our prayer.
or   Lord, in your mercy . . . Hear our prayer.
    (based on Jn 10:10)

62. *Name* found fellowship and a sense of community through *[specify activity]*_____. Grant him/her now the joy of fellowship and community with the saints.

    We pray to the Lord . . . Lord, hear our prayer.
or   Lord, in your mercy . . . Hear our prayer.

Outdoor Sports

63. God looked upon creation and saw that it was good. *Name* found the goodness of God in communing with nature while *[specify sport]*_____. May he/she now find eternal goodness and joy in heaven.

    We pray to the Lord . . . Lord, hear our prayer.
or   Lord, in your mercy . . . Hear our prayer.
    (based on Gn 1:31)

Spectator Sports/Sports Fan

64. *Name* was a faithful *[specify sport]*_____fan, and this love gave him/her a special bond to the *[specify team]*_____. May he/she now know the bond of being united with God forever.

    We pray to the Lord . . . Lord, hear our prayer.
or   Lord, in your mercy . . . Hear our prayer.

Water Sports

65. As *name* so often found life and refreshment *[specify water sport]* on/at/in the waters of *[specify body of water]*_____, may he/she now be refreshed in eternal life by Jesus, the Living Water.

We pray to the Lord . . . Lord, hear our prayer.

or   Lord, in your mercy . . . Hear our prayer.

(based on Jn 7:37-38)

Gardening

66. After the resurrection, you revealed yourself to Mary Magdalene in the garden, and she recognized you when you spoke her name. Now that you have called *name's* name, fill him/her with the joy of meeting you face to face in the garden of paradise.

We pray to the Lord . . . Lord, hear our prayer.

or   Lord, in your mercy . . . Hear our prayer.

(based on Jn 20:11-17)

67. You created the world as a garden for your children to tend and nurture. As *name* loved the beauty of earthly gardens, may he/she have the delight of walking with you in the splendors of paradise.

We pray to the Lord . . . Lord, hear our prayer.

or   Lord, in your mercy . . . Hear our prayer.

68. We knew *name* as an avid gardener. May the seeds of faith he/she sowed on earth now bloom in the garden of paradise.

We pray to the Lord . . . Lord, hear our prayer.

or   Lord, in your mercy . . . Hear our prayer.

Hand Crafts

69. *Name* took pleasure in creating *[specify]*_____. May he/she now delight in the company of God the Creator.

We pray to the Lord . . . Lord, hear our prayer.

or   Lord, in your mercy . . . Hear our prayer.

Reading

70. Through reading, *name* loved to explore the world and interact with the minds of others. May he/she now glory in exploring paradise and being united with the mind of God.

  We pray to the Lord . . . Lord, hear our prayer.
or Lord, in your mercy . . . Hear our prayer.

Ministry or Service
—Professional or Volunteer

4

Administrator, Manager, or Coordinator

Advocate for the Oppressed

Altar Server

Caretaker of Property

Catechist/Evangelism or Outreach Minister

Cook/Meal Preparation and Service Worker

Corporal Works of Mercy

Eucharistic Minister

Greeter

Lector

Musician, Choral or Instrumental

Parish Worker

Sacristan/Liturgical Environment Worker

Service Volunteer

Social Justice Advocate

Spiritual Works of Mercy

Third Order Member or Lay Missioner

Usher

Administrator, Manager, or Coordinator

71. As a/n *[specify]*_____, *name* exercised his/her talents in administration; may he/she now hear Christ say, "You were faithful in small matters . . . Come, share your Master's joy."

     We pray to the Lord . . . Lord, hear our prayer.
or   Lord, in your mercy . . . Hear our prayer.
     (based on Mt 25:14-15, 19-21)

Advocate for the Oppressed

72. During this life, *name* shared the burdens of the oppressed and worked that they might be freed from their distress. Grant that his/her work might bear much fruit and give him/her the eternal joy won for us by Jesus, our Liberator.

     We pray to the Lord . . . Lord, hear our prayer.
or   Lord, in your mercy . . . Hear our prayer.
     (based on Lk 4:16-18)
     See also prayer 90.

Altar Server

73. During his/her life, *name* ministered as a server at God's altar; in the heavenly Jerusalem may he/she continue to serve and worship the eternal God.

     We pray to the Lord . . . Lord, hear our prayer.
or   Lord, in your mercy . . . Hear our prayer.

Caretaker of Property

74. *Name* faithfully cared for *[object of care]*_____ during his/her life on earth; may he/she now experience God's enduring care for him/her.

     We pray to the Lord . . . Lord, hear our prayer.
or   Lord, in your mercy . . . Hear our prayer.

Catechist/Evangelism or Outreach Minister

75. As a/n *[specify role]*_____, *name* accompanied others in their search for God. May he/she now be accompanied to the celestial city by our prayers.

> We pray to the Lord . . . Lord, hear our prayer.

or   Lord, in your mercy . . . Hear our prayer.

76. May *name*, who devoted himself/herself to teaching the faith, now sit with joy at the feet of Jesus, who taught us to pray.

> We pray to the Lord . . . Lord, hear our prayer.

or   Lord, in your mercy . . . Hear our prayer.

> *See also prayer 91.*

Cook/Meal Preparation and Service Worker

77. *Name* prepared food to provide nourishment and hospitality to others; may he/she now relish the heavenly banquet in God's kingdom.

> We pray to the Lord . . . Lord, hear our prayer.

or   Lord, in your mercy . . . Hear our prayer.

> (based on 1 Pt 4:9-10)

Corporal Works of Mercy

> *See prayers 183-189.*

Eucharistic Minister

78. As *name* put the Gift of Finest Wheat into the hands of so many, may he/she now receive his/her eternal reward from the hands of God.

> We pray to the Lord . . . Lord, hear our prayer.

or   Lord, in your mercy . . . Hear our prayer.

> (based on Ps 147:14, JB)

79. The spiritually hungry often received the Eucharist from the hands of *name*. May the Lord now satisfy all his/her hungers at the eternal banquet of heaven.
> We pray to the Lord . . . Lord, hear our prayer.

or   Lord, in your mercy . . . Hear our prayer.
> (based on Ps 107:8-9)

Eucharistic Minister to the Homebound

80. The Bread of Life was often brought to the sick by *name*; may that celestial Bread now bring him/her to the eternal banquet.
> We pray to the Lord . . . Lord, hear our prayer.

or   Lord, in your mercy . . . Hear our prayer.
> (based on Jn 6:47-51)

Greeter

81. As a greeter, *name* welcomed the community of believers into God's house; may God now welcome *name* into his/her heavenly home.
> We pray to the Lord . . . Lord, hear our prayer.

or   Lord, in your mercy . . . Hear our prayer.

Lector

82. *Name* proclaimed your truth before men and women on earth; lead him/her now into the company of those who proclaim your glory forever in the new Jerusalem.
> We pray to the Lord . . . Lord, hear our prayer.

or   Lord, in your mercy . . . Hear our prayer.
> (based on Ps 40:1-2, 4, 6, 10-11)

83. As *name* acknowledged you before others, so now acknowledge him/her before your heavenly Father.
> We pray to the Lord . . . Lord, hear our prayer.

or   Lord, in your mercy . . . Hear our prayer.
> (based on Mt 10:32)

Musician, Choral or Instrumental

84. As *name* sang your praises here on earth, may he/she praise you forever with the choirs of heaven.

> We pray to the Lord . . . Lord, hear our prayer.
>
> *or*   Lord, in your mercy . . . Hear our prayer.
>
> (based on Ps 150)

85. Making music before the Lord was a part of *name's* life on earth. May he/she now join the harmonious voice of eternal glory.

> We pray to the Lord . . . Lord, hear our prayer.
>
> *or*   Lord, in your mercy . . . Hear our prayer.

86. *Name* loved to play the *[specify instrument]*_____be-fore the Lord. May he/she now be elated with the symphony of paradise.

> We pray to the Lord . . . Lord, hear our prayer.
>
> *or*   Lord, in your mercy . . . Hear our prayer.

Parish Worker

87. Jesus said, "The Son of Man did not come to be served, but to serve." *Name* served the parish by *[nature of service]*_____; may his/her humble service now be rewarded in heaven.

> We pray to the Lord . . . Lord, hear our prayer.
>
> *or*   Lord, in your mercy . . . Hear our prayer.
>
> (based on Mt 20:28)
>
> *See also prayer 229.*

Sacristan/Liturgical Environment Worker

88. Working in your sanctuary, *name* served you with love and reverence. Now in your tender compassion, draw him/her close to you and make him/her your own special possession.

> We pray to the Lord . . . Lord, hear our prayer.
>
> *or*   Lord, in your mercy . . . Hear our prayer.
>
> (based on Mal 3:16-17)

Service Volunteer

89. As a volunteer, *name* emulated Jesus in his/her life of service. May our Lord, the humble Servant, now welcome *name* into his kingdom.

> We pray to the Lord . . . Lord, hear our prayer.

or   Lord, in your mercy . . . Hear our prayer.
> *See also prayer 229.*

Social Justice Advocate

90. Jesus had a special love for the downtrodden and outcast. By *name's* advocacy for *[specify]*_____, he/she did the Lord's work. May he/she now receive his/her just reward.

> We pray to the Lord . . . Lord, hear our prayer.

or   Lord, in your mercy . . . Hear our prayer.
> (based on Lk 4:18-21)
> *See also prayer 72.*

Spiritual Works of Mercy

Converting the Sinner

91. *Name's* deep faith in God was a means for many to come to know the Lord. In the same way that he/she brought others to Christ, may we live in a way that draws others to our Savior.

> We pray to the Lord . . . Lord, hear our prayer.

or   Lord, in your mercy . . . Hear our prayer.
> *See also prayers 75-76.*

Converting the Sinner; A Priest/Confessor

92. For those who sought to deepen their conversion to Christ, Fr. *name* was often the means of grace. May we continue to foster his spirit of reconciliation through our lives.

We pray to the Lord . . . Lord, hear our prayer.

or   Lord, in your mercy . . . Hear our prayer.

Instructing the Ignorant

93. Like Jesus, *name* taught more than information; he/she taught values by which to live. May he/she now rejoice in the presence of the Master, the source of all truth and goodness.

We pray to the Lord . . . Lord, hear our prayer.

or   Lord, in your mercy . . . Hear our prayer.

See also prayers 50-51.

Counseling the Doubtful

94. *Name* was someone to whom many turned in times of spiritual struggle. May he/she be greeted at the gate of heaven by Jesus, the Wonderful-Counselor.

We pray to the Lord . . . Lord, hear our prayer.

or   Lord, in your mercy . . . Hear our prayer.

(based on Is 9:5)

See also prayer 107.

Comforting the Sorrowful

95. By his/her *[writing notes/making phone calls/taking time to visit, etc.]*, *name* was an instrument of the consolation of God, touching many who were weighed down by burdens and saddened by grief. May we in our own lives continue his/her work of comforting the sorrowful.

We pray to the Lord . . . Lord, hear our prayer.

or   Lord, in your mercy . . . Hear our prayer.

Bearing Wrongs Patiently

96. *Name* bore wrongs patiently, turning the other cheek as Jesus called us to do. May we imitate him/her in this challenging expression of mercy.

> We pray to the Lord . . . Lord, hear our prayer.

or   Lord, in your mercy . . . Hear our prayer.

> (based on Mt 5:39)

Forgiving Injuries

97. *Name* endeared himself/herself to others by being one who was willing to forgive quickly. May we imitate him/her in living out the scripture, "As the Lord has forgiven you, so must you also do."

> We pray to the Lord . . . Lord, hear our prayer.

or   Lord, in your mercy . . . Hear our prayer.

> (based on Col 3:12-13)

98. As part of our community of faith, *name* prayed in the Lord's Prayer to forgive and to be forgiven. May he/she now be received into the arms of our forgiving God.

> We pray to the Lord . . . Lord, hear our prayer.

or   Lord, in your mercy . . . Hear our prayer.

Praying for the Living and the Dead

99. James tells us, "The heartfelt prayer of someone upright works very powerfully." *Name* was a powerful intercessor for many on life's journey. May our prayers accompany *name* on his/her journey to heaven.

> We pray to the Lord . . . Lord, hear our prayer.

or   Lord, in your mercy . . . Hear our prayer.

> (based on Jas 5:16, NJB)

Third Order Member or Lay Missioner

See prayer 112.

Usher

100. As an usher, *name* helped many to find a place at the eucharistic banquet; may he/she now find a place at the banquet of heaven.

      We pray to the Lord . . . Lord, hear our prayer.

or   Lord, in your mercy . . . Hear our prayer.

5

Special Place in the Faith Community

Acquainted With Grief

Faithful Witnesses

Eucharistic Devotion

Acquainted With Grief

One Faithful in the Face of Suffering

101. Through his/her suffering, *name* shared in the pattern of Christ's death. Now may he/she know the power and fullness of Christ's resurrection.

> We pray to the Lord . . . Lord, hear our prayer.

or   Lord, in your mercy . . . Hear our prayer.
> (based on Phil 3:10-11)
> *See also prayers 114, 237.*

One Who Suffered for the Sake of the Gospel
> *See prayers 132, 158.*

One Who Offered Suffering as Prayer for the World
> *See prayer 132.*

One Who Was Unjustly Accused
> *See prayer 236.*

One Who Suffered Greatly Physically, Emotionally, or Spiritually
> *See prayers 113, 134-135, 237.*

Faithful Witnesses

One Committed to Intercessory Prayer
> *See prayer 99.*

One Whose Daily Living Was a Strong Christian Witness

102. Through the way *name* lived out his/her daily life, he/she gave witness to others about God. May God embrace him/her with love and welcome him/her now into the company of faithful disciples.

We pray to the Lord . . . Lord, hear our prayer.

or   Lord, in your mercy . . . Hear our prayer.

103. St. Paul says, "I have finished the race; I have kept the faith." *Name* was noted for his/her Christian witness and love of his/her faith; may he/she now receive the crown which has been reserved for him/her.

We pray to the Lord . . . Lord, hear our prayer.

or   Lord, in your mercy . . . Hear our prayer.

(based on 2 Tm 4:6-8)

A Faithful Seeker
See prayer 120.

An Invisible Servant

104. *Name* was a person who served quietly, but you have seen all that he/she did in secret. Grant him/her now the recognition and reward he/she deserves as your invisible servant.

We pray to the Lord . . . Lord, hear our prayer.

or   Lord, in your mercy . . . Hear our prayer.

(based on Mt 6:1-4)

A Life-Giving Presence to Others

105. *Name* has been a person of salt and light among us. May his/her example continue to guide us and may his/her light shine brightly before you in the heavenly city.

We pray to the Lord . . . Lord, hear our prayer.

or   Lord, in your mercy . . . Hear our prayer.

(based on Mt 5:13-16)

One Who Lived in Preparedness for Christ's Coming
See prayers 181-182, 196.

One Who Loved Scripture
See prayers 157, 208-209.

One Who Put Faith Into Action

106. St. Paul gave thanks for those who showed their "faith in action, worked for love, and persevered through hope." *Name* put his/her faith into action by *[specify]*_____; may he/she now receive the fulfillment of his/her hope, the fullness of God's love.

      We pray to the Lord . . . Lord, hear our prayer.
or   Lord, in your mercy . . . Hear our prayer.
      (based on 1 Thes 1:2-3, JB)

A Person of Quiet Faith
See prayers 120-121.

A Spiritual Guide for Others

107. In guiding others to God, *name* was a channel of the Holy Spirit. May the Spirit of God now breathe the fullness of eternal life into him/her.

      We pray to the Lord . . . Lord, hear our prayer.
or   Lord, in your mercy . . . Hear our prayer.
      (based on Wis 7:25-27, JB)
      See also prayer 94.

Eucharistic Devotion

One Devoted to Eucharistic Adoration
See prayer 211.

One Devoted to the Reception of Christ in the Eucharist
See prayers 213-218.

Circumstance of Death

A Life Laid Down for Another

See prayers 128-129, 228.

One Courageous in the Face of Death

See prayer 151.

A Tragic Death

See prayer 138.

A Tragic, Premature Death

See prayers 116, 194-195.

Suicide

108. Lord, you are full of tenderness and compassion. Have mercy upon *name*, our loved one, who in a time of pain sought his/her relief in death.

    We pray to the Lord . . . Lord, hear our prayer.

or   Lord, in your mercy . . . Hear our prayer.

109. Lord, you are our light in the darkness and our hope when tempted to despair. We pray for *name*, who saw more hope in death than in life. In your great love, receive him/her into your gentle, healing presence.

    We pray to the Lord . . . Lord, hear our prayer.

or   Lord, in your mercy . . . Hear our prayer.

110. We feel we have failed *name* by not being able to draw him/her into renewed life and hope. May the Lord grant us compassion in our remorse and comfort in the knowledge that *name* will be welcomed into the presence of our loving God.

    We pray to the Lord . . . Lord, hear our prayer.

or   Lord, in your mercy . . . Hear our prayer.

A Sudden, Unexpected Death

See prayers 194-195.

After a Long Decline in Health

See prayer 147.

One Who Experienced Pain

See prayer 164.

When the Deceased Has Held Off Death Until an Event or Reconciliation Has Come to Closure

See prayers 239-240.

Part Two

Prayers Based on the Readings From the Lectionary for Funerals

Old Testament Readings

New Testament Readings

Gospel Readings

Burial of Baptized Children

Burial of Non-Baptized Children

Old Testament Readings

Jb 19:1, 23-27

111. Like Job, *name* longed to see God with his/her own eyes; may that desire now be fulfilled.

      We pray to the Lord . . . Lord, hear our prayer.

or   Lord, in your mercy . . . Hear our prayer.

Wis 3:1-9

112. As *name* made his/her life an offering to God, may we rejoice that God has accepted this sacrificial offering in taking *name* to himself.

      We pray to the Lord . . . Lord, hear our prayer.

or   Lord, in your mercy . . . Hear our prayer.

113. May our pain be lessened by our trust that *name's* soul is in the hand of God and now no torment shall touch him/her.

      We pray to the Lord . . . Lord, hear our prayer.

or   Lord, in your mercy . . . Hear our prayer.

114. *Name's* faith made him/her courageous in the face of his/her suffering; may his/her courageous example strengthen us now that he/she has gone home to the Lord.

      We pray to the Lord . . . Lord, hear our prayer.

or   Lord, in your mercy . . . Hear our prayer.

115. May we who mourn *name's* death trust that God continues to abide with us and care for us in our loss.

      We pray to the Lord . . . Lord, hear our prayer.

or   Lord, in your mercy . . . Hear our prayer.

Wis 4:7-15

116. May those of us who have seen this tragedy come to understand how, before God, fullness of life can be attained in so short a time.

      We pray to the Lord . . . Lord, hear our prayer.

or   Lord, in your mercy . . . Hear our prayer.

Is 25:6a, 7-9

117. May the weighty veil of death be lifted from our eyes that we may see the God who has saved us.

> We pray to the Lord . . . Lord, hear our prayer.

or   Lord, in your mercy . . . Hear our prayer.

118. During his/her life, *name* looked to Jesus as his/her Savior; may we rejoice that he/she is now able to see the God who has saved him/her.

> We pray to the Lord . . . Lord, hear our prayer.

or   Lord, in your mercy . . . Hear our prayer.

119. May the Lord God wipe away the tears from our faces as we look to him who has saved us.

> We pray to the Lord . . . Lord, hear our prayer.

or   Lord, in your mercy . . . Hear our prayer.

Lam 3:17-26

120. During his/her life, *name* faithfully sought God. May he/she now rejoice in the presence of God whom he/she has found.

> We pray to the Lord . . . Lord, hear our prayer.

or   Lord, in your mercy . . . Hear our prayer.

121. *Name* lived his/her life with hope in the daily renewal of God's great mercy. May he/she now rejoice in the inexhaustible love of God.

> We pray to the Lord . . . Lord, hear our prayer.

or   Lord, in your mercy . . . Hear our prayer.

Dn 12:1-3

122. May the wisdom of *name*, which guided us during his/her life, continue to shine brightly in our lives.

> We pray to the Lord . . . Lord, hear our prayer.

or   Lord, in your mercy . . . Hear our prayer.

2 Mc 12:43-46

123. May *name* receive the splendid reward that awaits those who have gone to rest in godliness.

> We pray to the Lord . . . Lord, hear our prayer.

or   Lord, in your mercy . . . Hear our prayer.

New Testament Readings

Acts 10:34-36, 42-43

124. That *name* receive forgiveness of his/her sins as the fruit of his/her belief in Christ Jesus.

> We pray to the Lord . . . Lord, hear our prayer.

or   Lord, in your mercy . . . Hear our prayer.

125. During his/her life, *name* revered God and tried to act uprightly; may the Lord now accept him/her into his eternal embrace.

> We pray to the Lord . . . Lord, hear our prayer.

or   Lord, in your mercy . . . Hear our prayer.

126. *Name* was a faithful witness of God and ate and drank with us at God's altar; may his/her example inspire us to grow in our Christian witness.

> We pray to the Lord . . . Lord, hear our prayer.

or   Lord, in your mercy . . . Hear our prayer.

Rom 5:5-11

127. May we grow in our belief that *name* has now received reconciliation through our Lord Jesus Christ.

> We pray to the Lord . . . Lord, hear our prayer.

or   Lord, in your mercy . . . Hear our prayer.

128. Like Jesus, *name* found the courage to lay down his/her life for another. May his/her example give us the courage to sacrifice ourselves for others.

       We pray to the Lord . . . Lord, hear our prayer.

or   Lord, in your mercy . . . Hear our prayer.

129. In reaching out to one still helpless, *name* died. May we be inspired by this example of sacrificial love.

       We pray to the Lord . . . Lord, hear our prayer.

or   Lord, in your mercy . . . Hear our prayer.

Rom 5:17-21

130. May we rejoice that, where there was sin, God's grace has overflowed and brought *name* to eternal life.

       We pray to the Lord . . . Lord, hear our prayer.

or   Lord, in your mercy . . . Hear our prayer.

Rom 6:3-4, 8-9

131. May we grow in faith that *name* has risen with Christ to newness of life.

       We pray to the Lord . . . Lord, hear our prayer.

or   Lord, in your mercy . . . Hear our prayer.

Rom 8:14-23

132. *Name* united his/her sufferings to those of Christ for the redemption of the world. Now freed from his/her suffering, may he/she share in the glory of the children of God.

       We pray to the Lord . . . Lord, hear our prayer.

or   Lord, in your mercy . . . Hear our prayer.

133. May *name* join Christ in the inheritance which is ours as children of God.

       We pray to the Lord . . . Lord, hear our prayer.

or   Lord, in your mercy . . . Hear our prayer.

134. Although *name's* sufferings were great, may they be nothing compared to the glory which God will reveal to him/her.

We pray to the Lord . . . Lord, hear our prayer.

or   Lord, in your mercy . . . Hear our prayer.

135. We all bore witness to *name's* great sufferings. Since he/she has suffered with Christ, may he/she also be glorified with him.

We pray to the Lord . . . Lord, hear our prayer.

or   Lord, in your mercy . . . Hear our prayer.

Rom 8:31b-35, 37-39

136. May we grow in faith that, even though we all have sins and shortcomings, even these will not separate us from a loving God who calls us his chosen ones.

We pray to the Lord . . . Lord, hear our prayer.

or   Lord, in your mercy . . . Hear our prayer.

137. May we join our prayers for *name* to those of Jesus, who intercedes for us.

We pray to the Lord . . . Lord, hear our prayer.

or   Lord, in your mercy . . . Hear our prayer.

138. In this time of anguish, may we who mourn be comforted by the fact that nothing can separate us from the love of God.

We pray to the Lord . . . Lord, hear our prayer.

or   Lord, in your mercy . . . Hear our prayer.

Rom 14:7-9, 10b-12

139. *Name*, in his/her long life, trusted that all things are a part of God's providence. May we now take comfort that, in death, we can entrust him/her to the Lord.

We pray to the Lord . . . Lord, hear our prayer.

or   Lord, in your mercy . . . Hear our prayer.

140. While *name* lived, he/she was responsible to the Lord, and when he/she died, he/she died as his servant. May we follow his/her example.

We pray to the Lord . . . Lord, hear our prayer.

or   Lord, in your mercy . . . Hear our prayer.

141. May we grow in the heartfelt understanding that, whether we live or die, we are the Lord's.

       We pray to the Lord . . . Lord, hear our prayer.

or   Lord, in your mercy . . . Hear our prayer.

142. May *name*, who now stands before the judgment seat of God, give praise to the Lord forever.

       We pray to the Lord . . . Lord, hear our prayer.

or   Lord, in your mercy . . . Hear our prayer.

1 Cor 15:20-23, 24b-28

143. Christ was the firstfruits of those who have risen from the dead. May *name* rise with Christ, as one who belongs to him.

       We pray to the Lord . . . Lord, hear our prayer.

or   Lord, in your mercy . . . Hear our prayer.

144. In the humanity we share with Adam, we die. May we grow in faith that, in Christ, we shall be brought to eternal life.

       We pray to the Lord . . . Lord, hear our prayer.

or   Lord, in your mercy . . . Hear our prayer.

1 Cor 15:51-57

145. That we may be grateful to God that *name* has now been given victory over death through our Lord Jesus Christ.

       We pray to the Lord . . . Lord, hear our prayer.

or   Lord, in your mercy . . . Hear our prayer.

146. In his/her long life, *name* witnessed many changes. May we rejoice with him/her that his/her mortal life has been changed to immortality.

       We pray to the Lord . . . Lord, hear our prayer.

or   Lord, in your mercy . . . Hear our prayer.

147. *Name* experienced the failing of his/her corruptible body. Now freed from his/her mortality, may he/she rejoice in immortality.

       We pray to the Lord . . . Lord, hear our prayer.

or   Lord, in your mercy . . . Hear our prayer.

2 Cor 4:14-5:1

148. May we rejoice that *name* now lives in an eternal dwelling provided for him/her by our loving God.

We pray to the Lord . . . Lord, hear our prayer.

or   Lord, in your mercy . . . Hear our prayer.

149. In the face of the trauma of death, we ask the Lord to walk with us in faith since, with our human eyes, what we see is pain and separation.

We pray to the Lord . . . Lord, hear our prayer.

or   Lord, in your mercy . . . Hear our prayer.

2 Cor 5:1, 6-10

150. May we walk by faith and not by sight, knowing that, although *name* has left the body, he/she has gone home to the Lord.

We pray to the Lord . . . Lord, hear our prayer.

or   Lord, in your mercy . . . Hear our prayer.

151. *Name* was courageous in the face of death. May his/her example help us to be courageous in living out our lives, whatever circumstances we encounter.

We pray to the Lord . . . Lord, hear our prayer.

or   Lord, in your mercy . . . Hear our prayer.

Phil 3:20-21

152. May our prayers assist *name* to enter into his/her citizenship in heaven, promised by our Lord Jesus Christ.

We pray to the Lord . . . Lord, hear our prayer.

or   Lord, in your mercy . . . Hear our prayer.

153. May we grow in our belief that *name's* lowly body has been remade according to the pattern of Christ's glorified body.

We pray to the Lord . . . Lord, hear our prayer.

or   Lord, in your mercy . . . Hear our prayer.

1 Thes 4:13-18

154. *Name* is now with the Lord unceasingly. May we who loved him/her console one another with this message.

We pray to the Lord . . . Lord, hear our prayer.

or Lord, in your mercy . . . Hear our prayer.

155. In our grief, may we grow in our hope that we, too, shall rise from the dead and be with the Lord forever.

We pray to the Lord . . . Lord, hear our prayer.

or Lord, in your mercy . . . Hear our prayer.

2 Tm 2:8-13

156. In death, as in life, *name* depended on the Lord. May he/she now reign with the Lord in eternal glory.

We pray to the Lord . . . Lord, hear our prayer.

or Lord, in your mercy . . . Hear our prayer.

157. During his/her life, *name* loved the word of God. May he/she now fully enjoy the salvation promised us by God's Eternal Word, Jesus Christ.

We pray to the Lord . . . Lord, hear our prayer.

or Lord, in your mercy . . . Hear our prayer.

158. Like Paul, *name* suffered that the gospel might be preached/proclaimed. Because of his/her steadfast fidelity, may he/she now reign with Christ in glory.

We pray to the Lord . . . Lord, hear our prayer.

or Lord, in your mercy . . . Hear our prayer.

1 Jn 3:1-2

159. At this time of sorrow, may we see the great gift that God has given in making us his beloved children.

We pray to the Lord . . . Lord, hear our prayer.

or Lord, in your mercy . . . Hear our prayer.

1 Jn 3:14-16

160. By the example of his/her life, *name* helped us to understand what it means to love. May we live out this sacrificial love in our own lives.

We pray to the Lord . . . Lord, hear our prayer.

or Lord, in your mercy . . . Hear our prayer.

Rv 14:13

161. May the bounty of *name's* good works accompany him/her into the presence of the Lord.

We pray to the Lord . . . Lord, hear our prayer.

or Lord, in your mercy . . . Hear our prayer.

162. *Name* has now found rest from his/her labors. May his/her example inspire us to labor for the building up of God's kingdom.

We pray to the Lord . . . Lord, hear our prayer.

or Lord, in your mercy . . . Hear our prayer.

Rv 20:11-21:1

163. During life, *name* believed in the living God. May his/her name be recorded forever in the book of life.

We pray to the Lord . . . Lord, hear our prayer.

or Lord, in your mercy . . . Hear our prayer.

Rv 21:1-5a, 6b-7

164. In this life, *name* cried out in pain. May he/she now experience God's comforting presence in the new Jerusalem.

We pray to the Lord . . . Lord, hear our prayer.

or Lord, in your mercy . . . Hear our prayer.

165. May we who grieve and mourn the death of *name* look forward to the day when there shall be no more death or mourning.

We pray to the Lord . . . Lord, hear our prayer.

or Lord, in your mercy . . . Hear our prayer.

166. May we who grieve and mourn experience God's love wiping the tears from our eyes.

> We pray to the Lord . . . Lord, hear our prayer.

or   Lord, in your mercy . . . Hear our prayer.

167. For *name*, that he/she may drink from the spring of life-giving water forever.

> We pray to the Lord . . . Lord, hear our prayer.

or   Lord, in your mercy . . . Hear our prayer.

168. May *name* hear the Holy One on the throne speak these words: "I am your God and you are my son/daughter."

> We pray to the Lord . . . Lord, hear our prayer.

or   Lord, in your mercy . . . Hear our prayer.

Gospel Readings

Mt 5:1-12

169. We pray for those who mourn, that they may be comforted.

> We pray to the Lord . . . Lord, hear our prayer.

or   Lord, in your mercy . . . Hear our prayer.

170. For *name*, who was single-hearted in his/her love of God; may he/she now see his/her Savior face to face.

> We pray to the Lord . . . Lord, hear our prayer.

or   Lord, in your mercy . . . Hear our prayer.

171. May *name*, who was a peacemaker, now enjoy eternity as a child of God.

> We pray to the Lord . . . Lord, hear our prayer.

or   Lord, in your mercy . . . Hear our prayer.

172. During his/her life, *name* was persecuted for his/her faith. May he/she now experience the victory of the reign of God.

>   We pray to the Lord . . . Lord, hear our prayer.
or   Lord, in your mercy . . . Hear our prayer.

173. As *name* showed mercy and compassion to his/her sisters and brothers in life, may he/she now be encompassed in God's mercy.

>   We pray to the Lord . . . Lord, hear our prayer.
or   Lord, in your mercy . . . Hear our prayer.

174. *Name* was known to hunger and thirst for the things of God. May God now satisfy his/her hunger and quench his/her thirst.

>   We pray to the Lord . . . Lord, hear our prayer.
or   Lord, in your mercy . . . Hear our prayer.

175. On this earth, *name* was meek and gentle of heart. May he/she now enter into the inheritance promised by his/her gentle Savior.

>   We pray to the Lord . . . Lord, hear our prayer.
or   Lord, in your mercy . . . Hear our prayer.

176. In this life, *name* was humble in spirit. May he/she now enter into the reign of God.

>   We pray to the Lord . . . Lord, hear our prayer.
or   Lord, in your mercy . . . Hear our prayer.

Mt 11:25-30

177. *Name* had a simple, childlike faith in Jesus. May Jesus now reveal to *name* the fullness of the Father's love.

>   We pray to the Lord . . . Lord, hear our prayer.
or   Lord, in your mercy . . . Hear our prayer.

178. During his/her life, *name* entrusted himself/herself to the Lord's care. May Jesus now present this gift of his/her life to the Father.

>   We pray to the Lord . . . Lord, hear our prayer.
or   Lord, in your mercy . . . Hear our prayer.

179. You invited all those who labor and are burdened to come to you; now that *name* has released his/her earthly burdens into your hands, may he/she enjoy eternal rest.

      We pray to the Lord . . . Lord, hear our prayer.

or   Lord, in your mercy . . . Hear our prayer.

180. May Jesus, whose yoke is easy and whose burden is light, grant eternal rest to *name*.

      We pray to the Lord . . . Lord, hear our prayer.

or   Lord, in your mercy . . . Hear our prayer.

Mt 25:1-13

For a woman

181. Jesus reminds us, "Stay awake, for you know neither the day nor the hour." *Name* was vigilant in preparing to meet her heavenly Bridegroom. May her Bridegroom now welcome her into the wedding feast of heaven.

      We pray to the Lord . . . Lord, hear our prayer.

or   Lord, in your mercy . . . Hear our prayer.

For a man

182. Jesus reminds us, "Stay awake, for you know neither the day nor the hour." *Name* was vigilant in preparing to meet his Savior. May Jesus now welcome him into the wedding feast of heaven.

      We pray to the Lord . . . Lord, hear our prayer.

or   Lord, in your mercy . . . Hear our prayer.

Mt 25:31-46: The Corporal Works of Mercy

Feeding the Hungry

183. On earth *name* worked to feed the hungry. Now, in paradise, feed him/her forever from the tree of life.

      We pray to the Lord . . . Lord, hear our prayer.

or   Lord, in your mercy . . . Hear our prayer.

Welcoming the Stranger

184. On earth *name* welcomed the stranger. Now welcome him/her into the community of the heavenly host.

> We pray to the Lord . . . Lord, hear our prayer.

or   Lord, in your mercy . . . Hear our prayer.

Clothing the Naked

185. On earth *name* worked to clothe the naked. Now, in heaven, clothe him/her in your own radiant splendor.

> We pray to the Lord . . . Lord, hear our prayer.

or   Lord, in your mercy . . . Hear our prayer.

Providing for the Other Needs of the Poor

186. Through *name's* acts of kindness, the poor had the good news preached to them. May he/she now enter the kingdom Jesus proclaimed.

> We pray to the Lord . . . Lord, hear our prayer.

or   Lord, in your mercy . . . Hear our prayer.

Caring for the Sick

187. By caring for the sick, *name* imitated Jesus' love. May he/she receive the heavenly reward of his/her compassion.

> We pray to the Lord . . . Lord, hear our prayer.

or   Lord, in your mercy . . . Hear our prayer.

Visiting the Imprisoned

188. Through *name's* visits with the imprisoned, others met Christ. May he/she now meet Christ face to face.

> We pray to the Lord . . . Lord, hear our prayer.

or   Lord, in your mercy . . . Hear our prayer.

Sheltering the Homeless

189. During his/her earthly life, *name* worked to provide shelter for the homeless; now shelter him/her forever in your Father's heavenly mansion.

> We pray to the Lord . . . Lord, hear our prayer.

or   Lord, in your mercy . . . Hear our prayer.

Mk 15:33-39, 16:1-6 (long form)
or   Mk 15:33-39 (short form)

190. *Name* experienced times of *[physical suffering/emotional pain/spiritual darkness]* as did Jesus on the cross; now may the veil of *[suffering/pain/darkness]* be rent so that he/she can see the face of God.

     We pray to the Lord . . . Lord, hear our prayer.

or   Lord, in your mercy . . . Hear our prayer.

191. The death of *name* has brought darkness into our lives. May the light of the resurrected Jesus bring us new hope.

     We pray to the Lord . . . Lord, hear our prayer.

or   Lord, in your mercy . . . Hear our prayer.

Lk 7:11-17

192. Like the people at Nain, we gather here to mourn a friend. Let us wipe away our tears and listen to Jesus say, "I bid you, arise."

     We pray to the Lord . . . Lord, hear our prayer.

or   Lord, in your mercy . . . Hear our prayer.

Lk 12:35-40

193. In knowing *name*, we have experienced many blessings. May we praise God because, through *name*'s life, God has visited his people.

     We pray to the Lord . . . Lord, hear our prayer.

or   Lord, in your mercy . . . Hear our prayer.

194. For *name*, death came as a thief in the night. We pray that he/she was blessed with the grace he/she needed to meet his/her Master.

     We pray to the Lord . . . Lord, hear our prayer.

or   Lord, in your mercy . . . Hear our prayer.

195. *Name* died before we were ready to let him/her go. From this tragedy, may we be encouraged to prepare for the Master's coming.

       We pray to the Lord . . . Lord, hear our prayer.
or   Lord, in your mercy . . . Hear our prayer.

196. *Name* had his/her lamp lit for the arrival of the Master. May he/she now experience the Master waiting upon him/her at the heavenly banquet.

       We pray to the Lord . . . Lord, hear our prayer.
or   Lord, in your mercy . . . Hear our prayer.

Lk 23:33, 39-43
197. For *name*, that Jesus' assurance of joining him in paradise will be fulfilled.

       We pray to the Lord . . . Lord, hear our prayer.
or   Lord, in your mercy . . . Hear our prayer.

198. Aware of our offenses, we pray with the good thief, "Jesus, remember us when you come into your kingdom."

       We pray to the Lord . . . Lord, hear our prayer.
or   Lord, in your mercy . . . Hear our prayer.

Lk 23:44-46, 50, 52-53; 24:1-6a (long form)
199. May we who mourn *name*'s death come to understand that he/she is not here, but has been raised up.

       We pray to the Lord . . . Lord, hear our prayer.
or   Lord, in your mercy . . . Hear our prayer.

200. For us who mourn, that our lives may be a search for the Living One who will raise us from the dead.

       We pray to the Lord . . . Lord, hear our prayer.
or   Lord, in your mercy . . . Hear our prayer.

Lk 23:44-46, 50, 52-53 (short form)

201. As a community of faith, we gather to commend the spirit of *name* into the hands of God.

　　　We pray to the Lord . . . Lord, hear our prayer.

or　　Lord, in your mercy . . . Hear our prayer.

202. May we who mourn *name's* loss commend our spirits into the hands of God at the time of our own death.

　　　We pray to the Lord . . . Lord, hear our prayer.

or　　Lord, in your mercy . . . Hear our prayer.

Lk 24:13-35 (long form)

203. May we, like the disciples on the road to Emmaus, meet Christ in our grieving, and, through the scriptures and the breaking of the bread, may he give us new hope.

　　　We pray to the Lord . . . Lord, hear our prayer.

or　　Lord, in your mercy . . . Hear our prayer.

204. We mourn the physical departure of *name* from us. At this time of sadness, may we invite Christ to stay with us.

　　　We pray to the Lord . . . Lord, hear our prayer.

or　　Lord, in your mercy . . . Hear our prayer.

205. By *name's* Christian witness/example, he/she declared that Jesus is alive. We pray that when others see us they may experience the risen Lord.

　　　We pray to the Lord . . . Lord, hear our prayer.

or　　Lord, in your mercy . . . Hear our prayer.

Lk 24:13-16, 28-35 (short form)

206. As we gather around this altar to celebrate the breaking of the bread, may we come to a deeper knowledge of Jesus who has truly risen.

　　　We pray to the Lord . . . Lord, hear our prayer.

or　　Lord, in your mercy . . . Hear our prayer.

207. *Name* had a deep awareness of Christ in the Eucharist. From the example of his/her life, may our eyes be opened to see Christ more clearly in the breaking of the bread.

      We pray to the Lord . . . Lord, hear our prayer.
or   Lord, in your mercy . . . Hear our prayer.

Jn 5:24-29

208. *Name* was open to God's word and believed in Jesus' promise of eternal life. May he/she now experience the fulfillment of that promise to the resurrection of life.

      We pray to the Lord . . . Lord, hear our prayer.
or   Lord, in your mercy . . . Hear our prayer.

209. Through sacred scripture, *name* heard the voice of the Son of God. May we be reminded of the promise that "those who hear will live."

      We pray to the Lord . . . Lord, hear our prayer.
or   Lord, in your mercy . . . Hear our prayer.

Jn 6:37-40

210. Jesus promises that no one who comes to him will ever be rejected. May *name* now experience the embrace of our loving Father.

      We pray to the Lord . . . Lord, hear our prayer.
or   Lord, in your mercy . . . Hear our prayer.

211. *Name* spent long hours looking upon the Son and believing in him. May he/she experience the joy of being raised up on the last day.

      We pray to the Lord . . . Lord, hear our prayer.
or   Lord, in your mercy . . . Hear our prayer.

212. *Name* believed in Jesus and his promise of eternal life. May he/she now experience the fullness of eternal life in heaven.

      We pray to the Lord . . . Lord, hear our prayer.
or   Lord, in your mercy . . . Hear our prayer.

Jn 6:51-58

213. *Name* faithfully received the "living bread come down from heaven." May his/her reception of that Living Bread now raise him/her up to heaven.

> We pray to the Lord . . . Lord, hear our prayer.

or   Lord, in your mercy . . . Hear our prayer.

214. *Name* was a faithful participant in the Eucharistic banquet. May he/she now join Jesus at the eternal banquet of heaven.

> We pray to the Lord . . . Lord, hear our prayer.

or   Lord, in your mercy . . . Hear our prayer.

215. May we who gather around this altar, to eat and drink of the Body and Blood of Christ, be comforted in our belief that we will be raised up with *name* on the last day.

> We pray to the Lord . . . Lord, hear our prayer.

or   Lord, in your mercy . . . Hear our prayer.

216. As the reception of Holy Communion united us with *name* in the community of faith on this earth, so may we be united with *name* in the communion of saints in heaven.

> We pray to the Lord . . . Lord, hear our prayer.

or   Lord, in your mercy . . . Hear our prayer.

217. Through the reception of Holy Communion, *name* remained in Christ and Christ remained in him/her. May we always remember that, through the Eucharist, we continue to be united to *name* in God.

> We pray to the Lord . . . Lord, hear our prayer.

or   Lord, in your mercy . . . Hear our prayer.

218. *Name* was nourished by the Bread from Heaven. May he/she now enjoy the everlasting inheritance promised to those who feed upon this heavenly Food.

> We pray to the Lord . . . Lord, hear our prayer.

or   Lord, in your mercy . . . Hear our prayer.

Jn 11:17-27 (long form)

219. May the Lord use us as a means of grace to comfort *name's* family in their loss.

> We pray to the Lord . . . Lord, hear our prayer.

or   Lord, in your mercy . . . Hear our prayer.

220. Just as the Jewish friends of Martha and Mary came to comfort them, may we gather around the family of *name* to support them at this time of grief.

> We pray to the Lord . . . Lord, hear our prayer.

or   Lord, in your mercy . . . Hear our prayer.

Jn 11:21-27 (short form)

221. May we imitate Martha in her firm belief in Jesus, the Resurrection and the Life.

> We pray to the Lord . . . Lord, hear our prayer.

or   Lord, in your mercy . . . Hear our prayer.

222. In our anguish we question why our brother/sister *name* had to die. May we be like Martha and find in Jesus hope and courage to go on.

> We pray to the Lord . . . Lord, hear our prayer.

or   Lord, in your mercy . . . Hear our prayer.

Jn 11:32-45

223. In our grief and tears may we see the compassion that Jesus has for those who mourn.

> We pray to the Lord . . . Lord, hear our prayer.

or   Lord, in your mercy . . . Hear our prayer.

224. At the death of his friend, Jesus wept. As we grieve, may God give us the grace to be able to shed our tears with one another.

> We pray to the Lord . . . Lord, hear our prayer.

or   Lord, in your mercy . . . Hear our prayer.

225. In our search for an answer to the question, "Why has this happened?" may we not lose hope that, if we believe, we will see the glory of God.

      We pray to the Lord . . . Lord, hear our prayer.
or   Lord, in your mercy . . . Hear our prayer.

226. As Lazarus' family and friends wept, Jesus wept with them. May we be consoled by the fact that Christ shares our suffering with us.

      We pray to the Lord . . . Lord, hear our prayer.
or   Lord, in your mercy . . . Hear our prayer.

227. Just as Jesus had confidence that the Father heard him, may we trust that God hears us when we call out from the depth of our grief and pain.

      We pray to the Lord . . . Lord, hear our prayer.
or   Lord, in your mercy . . . Hear our prayer.

Jn 12:23-28 (long form)

228. At the moment of crisis, *name* did not allow the cost of the sacrifice to deter him/her from continuing to give. In this, may we see reflected the sacrifice of Christ.

      We pray to the Lord . . . Lord, hear our prayer.
or   Lord, in your mercy . . . Hear our prayer.

Jn 12:23-26 (short form)

229. *Name* faithfully served this community of faith. May he/she now receive the honor accorded to one who serves at the side of Christ.

      We pray to the Lord . . . Lord, hear our prayer.
or   Lord, in your mercy . . . Hear our prayer.

230. *Name* loved the things of heaven more than those of this earth. May he/she now share the joy of eternal life in the presence of the living God.

      We pray to the Lord . . . Lord, hear our prayer.

or   Lord, in your mercy . . . Hear our prayer.

231. *Name* was a faithful servant, sowing many good seeds during his/her life. May his/her death be an occasion for us to see and celebrate the good fruit of his/her life.

      We pray to the Lord . . . Lord, hear our prayer.

or   Lord, in your mercy . . . Hear our prayer.

Jn 14:1-6

232. At this time of loss, may our faith in God calm our troubled hearts.

      We pray to the Lord . . . Lord, hear our prayer.

or   Lord, in your mercy . . . Hear our prayer.

233. May we trust in Jesus' assurance that not only has he prepared a place for *name*, but he will also prepare a dwelling place for us in his Father's house.

      We pray to the Lord . . . Lord, hear our prayer.

or   Lord, in your mercy . . . Hear our prayer.

234. *Name* knew that the way to eternal life was through following Jesus. May we share his/her faith in Jesus, the Way, the Truth, and the Life.

      We pray to the Lord . . . Lord, hear our prayer.

or   Lord, in your mercy . . . Hear our prayer.

Jn 17:24-26

235. May we grow in our belief that by passing through death we enter into the glory of the Lord's presence.

      We pray to the Lord . . . Lord, hear our prayer.

or   Lord, in your mercy . . . Hear our prayer.

Jn 19:17-18, 25-30

236. *Name* shared with Jesus the suffering of being unjustly accused. Through our prayers, we now hand his/her spirit over to our loving Father.

>   We pray to the Lord . . . Lord, hear our prayer.
> *or*   Lord, in your mercy . . . Hear our prayer.

237. Just as Jesus carried his cross by himself, so *name* felt the burden of suffering alone. May we rejoice that his/her earthly isolation is ended as he/she enters into the companionship of the saints.

>   We pray to the Lord . . . Lord, hear our prayer.
> *or*   Lord, in your mercy . . . Hear our prayer.

238. As Jesus entrusted his mother and John to one another, so, with the death of *name*, we are called to a deeper love and care for one another. May God show us the way.

>   We pray to the Lord . . . Lord, hear our prayer.
> *or*   Lord, in your mercy . . . Hear our prayer.

When the Deceased Has Held Off Death Until an Event or Reconciliation Has Come to Closure

Event

239. Just as Jesus had one thing he had to do before he could die, so *name* waited for *[specify event]*_____. With *name*, we now hand over his/her spirit to God.

>   We pray to the Lord . . . Lord, hear our prayer.
> *or*   Lord, in your mercy . . . Hear our prayer.

Reconciliation

240. Just as Jesus needed to bring John and his mother into a new relationship before he could die, so *name* waited until his/her loved ones were reconciled. May this relationship be as blessed as that of John and the Blessed Mother.

>   We pray to the Lord . . . Lord, hear our prayer.
> *or*   Lord, in your mercy . . . Hear our prayer.

Burial of Baptized Children

Rv 7:9-10, 15-17

241. At *name's* baptism, he/she was dressed in the white garment of Christ. May we trust that his/her passing from this life has brought him/her to God's throne and to the Lamb who died for him/her.

> We pray to the Lord . . . Lord, hear our prayer.

or Lord, in your mercy . . . Hear our prayer.

242. At *name's* baptism, he/she was brought into the communion of saints. May we find comfort as this communion welcomes him/her into their company before God's throne.

> We pray to the Lord . . . Lord, hear our prayer.

or Lord, in your mercy . . . Hear our prayer.

For a child who suffered

243. During *name's* brief life, he/she knew many hardships and sufferings. Now may the Lamb of God shepherd him/her to the springs of eternal life and peace.

> We pray to the Lord . . . Lord, hear our prayer.

or Lord, in your mercy . . . Hear our prayer.

Burial of Non-Baptized Children

Mk 15:33-46

244. With the death of *name*, the veil of our hearts has been rent. May love flow from the heart of Jesus to touch and heal us.

> We pray to the Lord . . . Lord, hear our prayer.

or   Lord, in your mercy . . . Hear our prayer.

245. As Pilot expressed disbelief that Jesus had died so soon, we can hardly believe that *name* has died so soon. In our struggle, may we be aware of God's comforting presence.

> We pray to the Lord . . . Lord, hear our prayer.

or   Lord, in your mercy . . . Hear our prayer.

246. Like Joseph of Arimathea, we have come to bury our loved one. May we also come to know in our hearts that death is not the end.

> We pray to the Lord . . . Lord, hear our prayer.

or   Lord, in your mercy . . . Hear our prayer.

Appendix

Form for Noting Readings and Compiling Intercessions for a Funeral Liturgy

Here we offer a form as an aid for pastoral staff in their preparation for funeral liturgies.

It is designed for noting selected scriptures and their page and reading numbers in the lectionary, as well as compiling prayers of the faithful from different locations. Thus, its use can assist in the process of integrating the prayers of the faithful with the scripture readings in a meaningful way.

Intercessions composed or adapted specifically for the particular liturgy can also be recorded here. Therefore, this form can enable the assisting minister to read prayers from various sources in a smooth sequence without the distraction of paging through and scanning a number of sources or loose notes.

Funeral Readings and Intercessions

Funeral of _____ Date: _____

Scriptures: Lectionary location:

    First reading _____ page ____ no. _____
    Psalm _____ page ____ no. _____
    Second reading _____ page ____ no. _____
    Gospel _____ page ____ no. _____

Intercessions: from *Order of Christian Funerals* (OCF) or *Blessed Are Those Who Mourn* (TWM)

___ OCF   ___ TWM   page ____ no. _____

_____

_____

_____

We pray to the Lord . . . Lord, hear our prayer.
or **Lord, in your mercy** . . . Hear our prayer.

___ OCF   ___ TWM   page ____ no. _____

_____

_____

_____

We pray to the Lord . . . Lord, hear our prayer.
or **Lord, in your mercy** . . . Hear our prayer.

___ OCF   ___ TWM   page ____ no. _____

_____

_____

_____

We pray to the Lord . . . Lord, hear our prayer.
or **Lord, in your mercy** . . . Hear our prayer.

Funeral of _____ **Date:** _____

Intercessions: from _Order of Christian Funerals_ **(OCF) or** _Blessed Are Those Who Mourn_ **(TWM)**

___ **OCF**   ___ **TWM**   **page** ____ **no.** _____

_____

_____

_____

We pray to the Lord . . . Lord, hear our prayer.
_or_ **Lord, in your mercy . . .** Hear our prayer.

___ **OCF**   ___ **TWM**   **page** ____ **no.** _____

_____

_____

_____

We pray to the Lord . . . Lord, hear our prayer.
_or_ **Lord, in your mercy . . .** Hear our prayer.

___ **OCF**   ___ **TWM**   **page** ____ **no.** _____

_____

_____

_____

We pray to the Lord . . . Lord, hear our prayer.
_or_ **Lord, in your mercy . . .** Hear our prayer.

___ **OCF**   ___ **TWM**   **page** ____ **no.** _____

_____

_____

_____

We pray to the Lord . . . Lord, hear our prayer.
_or_ **Lord, in your mercy . . .** Hear our prayer.

Appendix B

A Supplement for Vigil Services:
Scriptures and Meditations
Based on the Glorious Mysteries of
the Rosary

In many parishes, in addition to the vigil service provided by the *Order of Christian Funerals*, people still wish to make the rosary one of the prayer forms celebrated before the funeral. The following reflections are offered as an optional supplement, a way of integrating scripture with a beloved devotion. They are based on an early Dominican form of the Glorious Mysteries of the Rosary:

> The First Glorious Mystery, The Resurrection of Our Lord
> The Second Glorious Mystery, The Ascension of Our Lord Into Heaven
> The Third Glorious Mystery, The Descent of the Holy Spirit at Pentecost
> The Fourth Glorious Mystery, The Assumption of the Blessed Virgin
> The Fifth Glorious Mystery, The Second Coming of Christ

For each decade there are two alternatives of scripture readings with meditations from which one may choose.

First Reflection: The Resurrection of Our Lord

Option A

Scripture reading: *A reading from Matthew's Gospel:*

The angel spoke; and he said to the women, "There is no need for you to be afraid. I know you are looking for Jesus, who was crucified. He is not here, for he has risen, as he said he would" (Mt 28:5-6, JB).

[Pause.]

Meditation: We, too, look for one who is gone;
    we cannot, yet, let them go.
We must minister to them one more time,
    we must see them just once again.
But they are not here, among the dead . . .

The angel points beyond the sorrow of death to an
    amazing joy.
The searching women must look beyond
    death to life, and that is where we must look also.

Option B

Scripture reading: *A reading from the letter to the Ephesians:*

[But] God, who is rich in mercy, because of the great love he had for us, even when we were dead in our transgressions, brought us to life with Christ (by grace you have been saved), raised us up with him, and seated us with him in the heavens in Christ Jesus (Eph 2:4-6).

[Pause.]

Meditation: God has loved us greatly and has been merciful to *us* also . . .

How many times have we fallen,
    but he has reached out and raised us up?
Or have we been in darkness,
    and he has shined his light upon us?
These are resurrection experiences in our own lives . . .

May we trust in God for that day
    when he will lift us through the darkness of death
    into the loving light which is eternal life in
    Christ Jesus.

Second Reflection: The Ascension of Our Lord Into Heaven

Option A

Scripture reading: *A reading from Luke's Gospel:*

Then [Jesus] took them out as far as the outskirts of
    Bethany, and lifting up his hands he blessed them.
Now as he blessed them, he withdrew from them and
was carried up to heaven (Lk 24:50-51, JB).

[Pause.]

Meditation: "Lifting up his hands he blessed them."

Their last sight of Jesus, their last memory of him,
    was his holy, loving, and gentle blessing.
Let us grow in love and gentle strength
    so, when the time comes for us to leave this world,
we may leave those whom we love
    with the image of our blessing.

Option B

Scripture reading: *A reading from the letter to the Colossians:*

If then you were raised with Christ, seek what is above, where Christ is seated at the right hand of God. Think of what is above, not of what is on earth. When Christ your life appears, then you too will appear with him in glory (Col 3:1-2, 4).

[Pause.]

Meditation: We are called to be *in* this world, but not *of* it,
        to see our lives through the eyes of eternity.
Our time in this world is important,
        but it is only the beginning to our life
        which extends beyond death, forever.
May we always remember our true home
        and keep our hearts on heaven.

Third Reflection: The Descent of the Holy Spirit at Pentecost

Option A

Scripture reading: *A reading from the Acts of the Apostles:*

When Pentecost day came round, they had all met in one room, when suddenly they heard what sounded like a powerful wind from heaven, the noise of which filled the entire house in which they were sitting; and something appeared to them that seemed like tongues of fire; these separated and came to rest on the head of each of them. They were all filled with the Holy Spirit (Acts 2:1-4, JB).

[Pause.]

Meditation: Jesus was gone.

He had ascended and told them to "WAIT" and waiting is hard,
   especially waiting in the emptiness that comes
   from losing the presence of someone you love.

But into that void poured a new Spirit
   and the empowerment to live a new life out of a
      new birth.
Into the losses, the voids of our lives,
   may we invite the fullness of the mighty God
   who is the Spirit of new births and new beginnings.

Option B

Scripture reading: *A reading from the letter of Jude:*

You, my dear friends, must use your most holy faith as your foundation and build on that, praying in the Holy Spirit; keep yourselves within the love of God and wait for the mercy of our Lord Jesus Christ to give you eternal life (Jude 20-21, JB).

[Pause.]

Meditation: The disciples were fearful after Jesus' ascension.
What dangers would confront them, now that he was
gone?

But they clung to a raw faith in Jesus and his word,
a radical hope arising from his resurrection,
and a binding love for one another.

May faith, hope, and love sustain us also in our distress
and open our hearts to the Holy Spirit,
Renewer and Comforter.

Fourth Reflection: The Assumption of the Blessed Virgin

Option A

Scripture reading: *A reading from the first letter to the Corinthians:*

Now Christ has been raised from the dead, the first fruits of those who have fallen asleep. For since death came through a human being, the resurrection of the dead came also through a human being. For just as in Adam all die, so too in Christ shall all be brought to life, but each one in proper order: Christ the firstfruits; then, at his coming, those who belong to Christ (1 Cor 15:20-23).

[Pause.]

Meditation:

As Mary had held Jesus, gently and lovingly,
    at his birth and at his death,
so now *he* gathers *her* into his arms and carries her
    to heaven.
Such care, such tenderness, in the way they loved
    each other . . .

He had proceeded her in death and new life,
    and now he comes for her
    as he will come for *all* those who belong to him.
May we look forward to that day
when he gently and tenderly carries us to heaven.

Option B

Scripture reading: *A reading from the prophet Isaiah:*

The nations then will see your integrity,
all the kings your glory,
and you will be called by a new name,
one which the mouth of Yahweh will confer.
You are to be a crown of splendor in the hand of Yahweh,
a princely diadem in the hand of your God;
. . . you shall be called "My Delight"
. . . for Yahweh takes delight in you (Is 62:2-4, JB).

[Pause.]

Meditation: God had sent an angel to Mary unexpectedly one day.
He had called her to trust and to obedience.
He had given her care of an impossible child
     who had God as his Father and herself as his mother.
He had found favor with her; he had called her to
     a privileged place.
He had called her to joy, to miracle, to suffering, and
     to grief.
She was Mother of God and Mother of Sorrows.
She was called to heaven and she became his Delight.
May we follow her example . . . and someday know
     her joy.

Fifth Reflection: The Second Coming of Christ

Option A

Scripture reading: *A reading from the book of Revelation:*

Then I saw a new heaven and a new earth. The former heaven and the former earth had passed away, and the sea was no more. I also saw the holy city, a new Jerusalem, coming down out of heaven from God, pre-pared as a bride adorned for her husband. I heard a loud voice from the throne saying, "Behold, God's dwelling is with the human race. He will dwell with them and they will be his people and God himself will always be with them [as their God]. He will wipe every tear from their eyes, and there shall be no more death or mourning, wailing or pain, [for] the old order has passed away."
The one who sat on the throne said, "Behold, I make all things new." Then he said, "Write these words down, for they are trustworthy and true" (Rv 21:1-5).

[Pause.]

Meditation:

We, too, are called to a vision of new hope.
In this earthly life, with its grief and pain, its suffering
    and loss,
        death marks the limit of our vision,
        a horizon beyond which we cannot see.

But we are called by Christ to see past this darkness
    through the mist of our tears.
There is a dawn on the horizon—
        the dawn of a new heaven and a new earth
        where the resurrected Christ reigns victorious
        and makes all things new.

Option B

Scripture reading: *A reading from the second letter to the Thessalonians:*

We always pray for you, that our God may make you worthy of his calling and powerfully bring to fulfillment every good purpose and every effort of faith, that the name of our Lord Jesus may be glorified in you, and you in him, in accord with the grace of our God and Lord Jesus Christ (2 Thes 1:11-12).

[Pause.]

Meditation: When Christ comes again . . .
      this is the day when all the labor
      of grace and service is done at last.

All the good we have desired will be fulfilled.
All the work we have done in faith will be complete.

God will be glorified in his people
      and they will be glorified in him, forever.

Scripture Index

Old Testament

New Testament

Scripture passage   *Prayer number*

Prayer Index